Look - Book 4

By Viola & Zaida Stefano

The rights of Viola & Zaida Stefano to be identified as the authors of this work have been asserted by them in accordance with the **Copyright Amendment (Moral Rights) Act 2000.**

All rights reserved. Apart from any use as permitted by the authors & under the **Copyright Act 1968**, no part may be reproduced, copied, scanned, stored in a retrieval system, recorded, or shared, by any means or in any form, without prior written permission from the publisher.

A catalogue record of this book is available from the **National Library of Australia.**

ISBN: 978-0-6458056-7-3

Authors: Viola Stefano & Zaida Stefano
Illustrations, photographs, cover & internal designs: Zaida Stefano

Illustrations copyright © Zaida Stefano 2023
Design copyright © Zaida Stefano 2023
Photographs copyright © Zaida Stefano 2023

Disclaimer: The content presented in this book is meant for educational purposes only. The authors & publisher claim no accountability to any entity or person for any liability, damage, or loss caused or assumed to be caused directly or indirectly as a consequence of the application, use, or interpretation of the material in this book.

VeeZee Publications

Copyright © VeeZee Publications Pty Ltd 2023
First published in Australia in 2023
by VeeZee Publications Pty Ltd
veezeepublications.com

Learning made easy with

VeeZee!

- Focus Core words in 'Look - Book 4' and the 'Look' series
- Secondary Core words in 'Look - Book 4' and the 'Look' series
- Other secondary Core words in the 'Look' series but **NOT** in 'Look - Book 4'

Core Vocabulary used throughout **VeeZee Publications**				
I	want	can	stop	look
like	more	he	go	see
here	what	do	the	and
out	where	we	it	up
not	they	when	that	down
she	now	them	is	put
help	off	you	yes	on
turn	who	this	no	why
done	make	a	to	under
come	in	some	which	there
open	get	good	same	home

All Core word readers through the various series in VeeZee Publications have been developed around specific themes. The themed photos and illustrations present a backdrop for the Core words used in each book. Your students are exploring and interpreting the messages conveyed by these images. They are learning to consider the text in order to understand the images. They are therefore making links between images and the corresponding texts. You are using a range of Core words when discussing the photos and illustrations with your students, especially; who, what, where, when and why. The use of these 'question' words in discussion further reinforces their meanings and their associations with surrounding words. We recommend that students without a vision impairment also explore the readers designed for students with low vision. This will support interaction and discussion amongst the students. It is our hope that this will ultimately promote acceptance, understanding, compassion and teamwork, thus cultivating true inclusion.

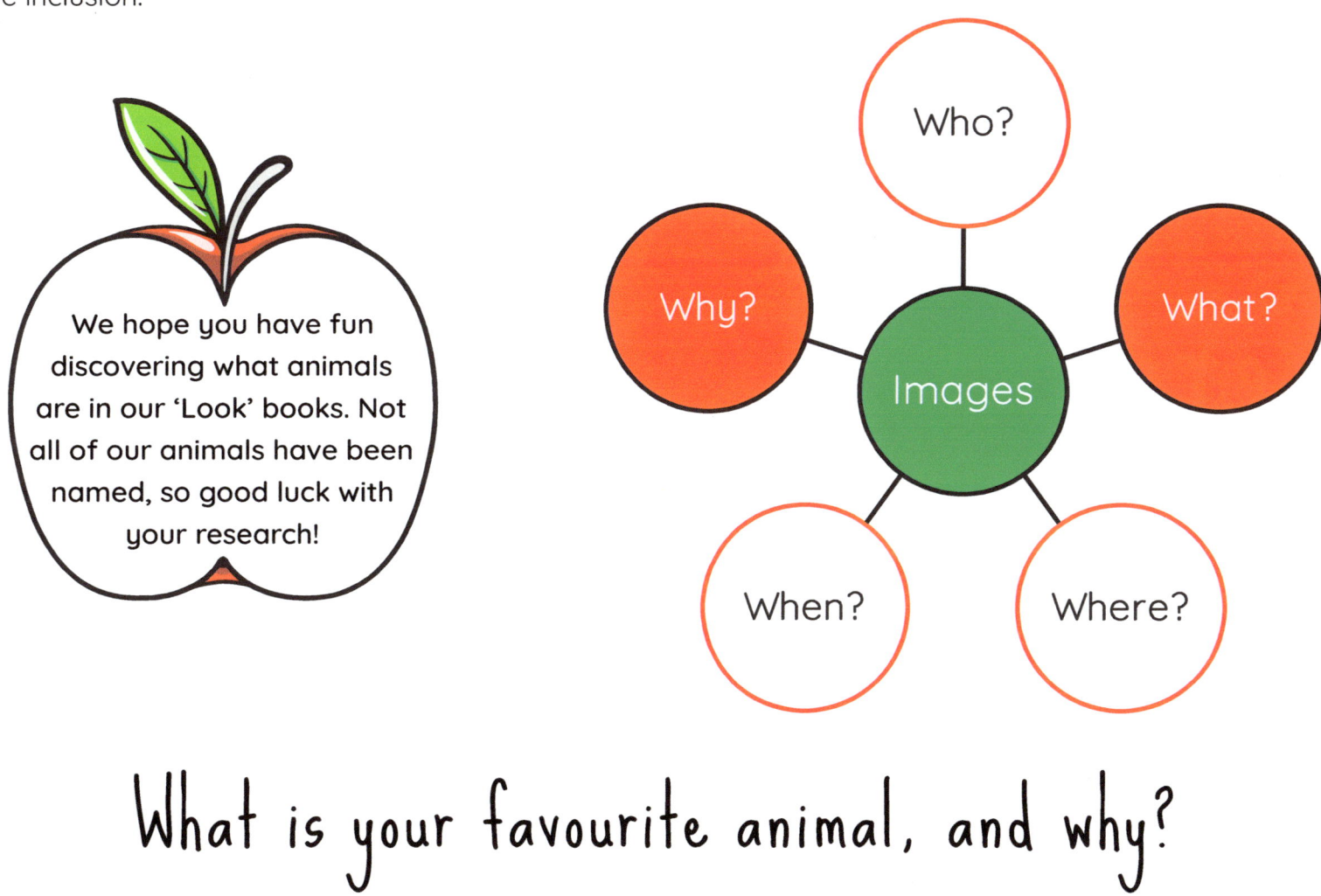

We hope you have fun discovering what animals are in our 'Look' books. Not all of our animals have been named, so good luck with your research!

What is your favourite animal, and why?

Look. I want to look at it here.

2

Look. I want to look at it there.

4

Look. I want to look at it down here.

Look. I want to look at it up there.

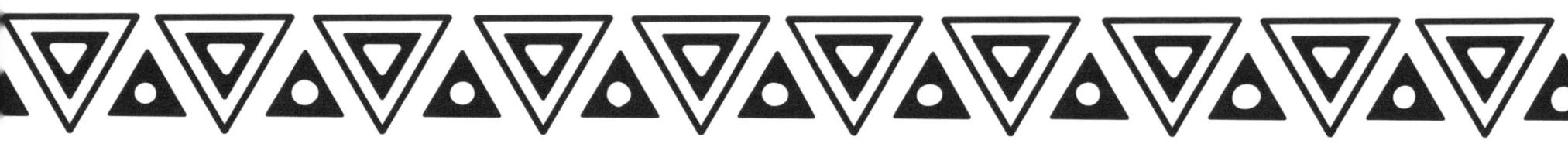

Look. I like that one.

10

Look. Do you like this one?

Come here mum. Look at it.

Come here dad. Look at that now.

We can turn left and look up at it.

We can turn right and look down at this.

No. Not there. Look here.

Look at them.

Look. Can you see them?

Look. I can see some more animals.

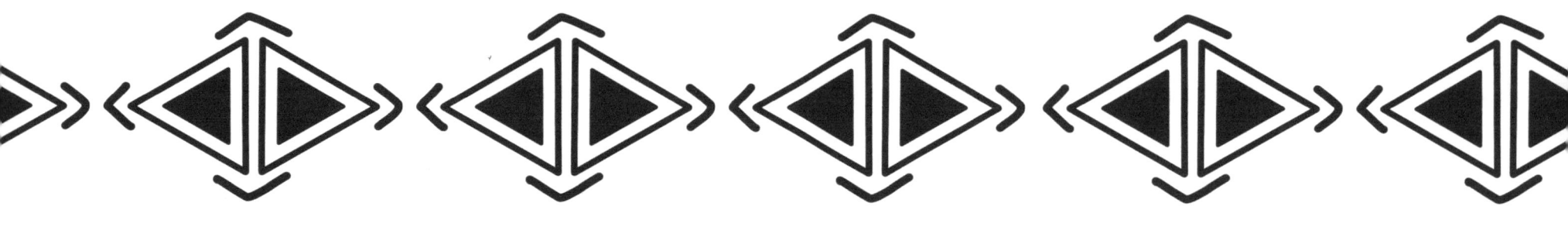

I can look at this animal now.

30

We can look at that animal now.

32

Words in this book

I	you	we
can	one	want
mum	dad	there
at	animals	not
turn	it	now
right	animal	more

Words in this book

like	to	up
see	and	down
look	here	no
do	this	that
them	come	some
	left	

Do you know the focus and secondary Core words: 'look', 'you' and 'there'? Read the words along each line.

look	there	you	there	look	you	there
there	you	there	look	look	there	you
there	look	there	look	there	you	there
look	there	you	look	you	there	look
there	you	look	look	there	you	there
look	there	look	you	there	you	look
there	look	there	there	look	there	you

Do you know the focus and secondary Core words in this book (refer to Core word table)? Find them along each line, point to them and say them. Read the other words too once you have pointed to the Core words.

look	you	more	like	we	can	here
not	turn	it	mum	I	look	that
now	look	no	to	dad	and	up
down	them	come	some	look	there	at
left	one	right	not	animal	more	like
and	look	this	that	like	down	look
you	look	here	animals	see	look	up

How many times did you read the word 'look'?

Make new words with '__at', e.g., 'flat'. Write sentences using these words.

We hope you had fun reading!

VeeZee Publications

Wait, there's more!

Visit our website for information about our range of readers & supporting products.

veezeepublications.com

www.ingramcontent.com/pod-product-compliance
Lightning Source LLC
Chambersburg PA
CBHW050853010526
44107CB00047BA/1596